Mrs. (

I well
always be grateful
for our friendship.
Love,

DH

.. Varonika

My Prayer Has Wings
EMOTION DEVOTIONAL

Varonika Hardman

ISBN: 978-0-9820700-0-0

Thomas Brown Publishing, LLC
Columbus, Georgia

About the Author

Minister Varonika Hardman is dedicated to teaching the Word of God beyond the church walls. She has been called to serve at a time when people need to hear God's Word more than ever and more often. The streets are calling more loudly than the Church! Young adults, children, unchurched, and other vulnerable souls are bombarded with more love, tolerance, and patience outside of the Church. Therefore, churches need to become more vigilant about evangelism, effective bible teaching, mentoring, and partnering with field experts for workshops on finance, health, professional growth – even classes for the children, such as public speaking or sign language.

It's time now for the Church to regain its rightful place as the center of our lives by ministering to the spiritual needs and also some of the practical needs of people.

In response to God's call, Minister Hardman has developed **Visionary Ministry,** which uses out-of-the box thinking, media, and technology to win and revive souls for Christ. As a minister and public relations consultant, she combines her calling with her professional skills to bring evangelism into the 21st Century.

Minister Hardman lives in Columbus, Georgia with her husband, Ryan, a professional musician, and their daughter.

To contact Minister Hardman for books or speaking engagements, email her at VisionaryMinistry@gmail.com.

Introduction

"Don't let the devil steal your joy." It was said often in our Baptist church in small town Florida. The almost weekly declaration can be linked to the 10th chapter of the Gospel of John, and more specifically, the 10th verse, when Jesus contrasts his purpose as the perfect shepherd to the goals of those who are not true shepherds.

The thief cometh not, but for to steal, and to kill, and to destroy: I am come that they might have life, and that they might have it more abundantly.

The silver-haired church mothers and deacons at my home church who made the almost weekly declaration were not well-read theologians with divinity degrees. They were strong men and women who held a hymn in their hearts and well-worn Bibles in their hands. As children, they learned to trust the Lord from even stronger Christian parents and grandparents who always gave God credit for seeing them through the storms of life.

We are His.

My Father, which gave them me, is greater than all; and no man is able to pluck them out of my Father's hand. (John 10:29)

John 10 serves to remind us that it the Lord who is the source of our victory. He is our leader, our protector and even our doorway. Jesus shares with us in John 10 that it is only through Him/by Him/with Him/on Him/in Him that we endure the valleys of life; enjoy the plateaus of life; and enter the rest of our lives with our Father in Heaven.

The devil cannot simply take us. However, we can give ourselves over to him. In tiny pieces each day, we can do that through our emotions.

Don't let the devil steal your joy. The good news is that the Word of God is our weapon. That's why the Word is called a sword (Ephesians 6:17 and Hebrews 4:12). On a daily basis, we are barraged by various emotions. Many of these emotions are needless feelings or even unchristian thoughts that are daggers from the thief who seeks to steal, kill and destroy.

The Emotion Devotional is the first book in the My Prayer Has Wings series.

Be blessed.
Varonika

How to use this book

Break the chains of negativity and usher in the Spirit! This book provides biblical references for 31 negative or unchristian feelings that you may experience within a month. The pages are not meant to be read in sequential order. Read the pages according to the emotion you are experiencing. Scriptural references are examined to show you that God wants you to rid yourself of feelings that do not benefit your spirit.

Following the scripture are questions and statements for meditation. Thinking and responding in your own handwriting should help you to plant good news in your heart and mind. A memory verse is included to serve as a foundation for your freedom prayer. At the end of the book, you will find a brief reminder of the fruit of the spirit – characteristics for Christians to embody.

This devotional is your reference to help you fight with two weapons: the words of the Lord and the truth of the Word in your own handwriting.

Keep this book handy. If the emotion returns in the future, go back to the entry and remind yourself of what God says about your feelings.

You are more than a conqueror! (Romans 8:7)

To my Father in Heaven:

Thank you for every yes and for every no. Thank you for every blessing and for every stumbling block. Thank you for my family and friends. Thank you, also, for those who have harmed me and for those who seek to harm me. I am who I am because of who YOU are. I am realizing that all things work together for my good because I love you and I have been called for a purpose. Thank you for Genesis through Revelation. Your Word is my light, my sword, and my pillow.

Table of Contents

Afraid

To Be Scared

To Dread

Fear is addressed quite often in the Bible. However, there are different connotations of the word. Sometimes, the word fear is used to mean "reverential awe" which is the meaning in the following verse:

Ye shall not therefore oppress one another; but thou shalt fear thy God: for I am the Lord your God. *Leviticus 25:17*

That is good fear. Christians must have the highest regard for the Lord and His Word. The fear that God speaks against is the other definition – being afraid or intimidated by someone or something.

Repeatedly, the Bible tells us not to fear. Our biblical heroes needed reminding. We benefit from reminders as well.

The author of Hebrews urges followers of Christ to believe in the safety of God.

So that we may boldly say, The Lord is my helper, and I will not fear what man shall do unto me. *Hebrews 13:6*

In the book of Isaiah, the prophet Isaiah speaks of imminent judgment for the enemies of God and encouragement to the people while they wait for the Lord's deliverance.

Say to them that are of a fearful heart, Be strong, fear not: behold, your God will come with vengeance, even God with a recompence; he will come and save you. *Isaiah 35:4*

Fear thou not; for I am with thee: be not dismayed; for I am thy God: I will strengthen thee; yea, I will help thee: yea, I will uphold thee with the right hand of my righteousness. *Isaiah 41:10*

Joshua puts captured enemies on display for all to see and tells the Israelites to expect the demise of more enemies.

And Joshua said unto them, Fear not, nor be dismayed, be strong and of good courage: for thus shall the Lord do to all your enemies against whom ye fight. *Joshua 10:25*

MEDITATION

It is normal to feel apprehensive or to dread something unexpected or even something negative that you do expect. I do not believe God is saying to us that we are not true Christians if we fear.

However, I believe our instructions are to resist the urge to give into fear. Fear is an unproductive emotion. Giving into fear does not demonstrate faith. Fear erodes faith.

What causes you to fear? Are you afraid of something right now?

_____

_____

_____

_____

_____

_____

_____

If faith is the core of Christianity, (Hebrews 11:6 tell us that it is impossible to please God without faith), then how dangerous is it for you to give into your fears?

_____

_____

_____

_____

_____

_____

MEMORY VERSE

The Lord is my light and my salvation; whom shall I fear? the Lord is the strength of my life; of whom shall I be afraid?
Psalm 27:1

+ Now, spend a few moments praying for freedom from your negative feeling.

Doubt

To Disbelieve

To Regard as Unlikely

Doubt is a sibling of fear. It is another example of diminishing faith. With God, all things are possible (Matthew 19:26). Christians are taught that God is omnipotent which means He holds ultimate power. Although He may not do something, He can do all things. No one else can be at the beginning, middle and end of all time.

God's hears all prayers but He knows who truly believes. So, as Christians we must not doubt the omnipotence of God or His promises.

Look at what can happen when God notices unbelief.

And the Lord spake unto Moses and Aaron, Because ye believed me not, to sanctify me in the eyes of the children of Israel, therefore ye shall not bring this congregation into the land which I have given them. *Numbers 20:12*

Jesus addressed the subject of doubt with the disciples.

Jesus answered and said unto them, Verily I say unto you, If ye have faith, and doubt not, ye shall not only do this which is done to the fig tree, but also if ye shall say unto this mountain, Be thou removed, and be thou cast into the sea; it shall be done. *Matthew 21:21*

It is mandatory that Christians refuse to doubt the goodness of God. He promises to reward us according to our faith.

Jesus explained the tremendous power of belief to Nicodemus. He that believeth on him is not condemned: but he that believeth not is condemned already, because he hath not believed in the name of the only begotten Son of God. *John 3:18*

MEDITATION

What do you regard as unlikely to happen in your life? Why?

_____

_____

_____

_____

If you have not received your desire, do you believe God's answer is "not yet" or "no?"

_____

_____

_____

_____

_____

Does an answer of "no" contradict Matthew 21:21?

_____

_____

_____

MEMORY VERSE

For verily I say unto you, That whosoever shall say unto this mountain, Be thou removed, and be thou cast into the sea; and shall not doubt in his heart, but shall believe that those things which he saith shall come to pass; he shall have whatsoever he saith. *Mark 11:23*

+ Now, spend a few moments praying for freedom from your negative feeling.

Worried

To be Uneasy

To Feel Troubled

In the book of Matthew, you will find that Jesus addresses worry with the original disciples. You and I are his modern-day disciples. The message is still true.

And why take ye thought for raiment? Consider the lilies of the field, how they grow; they toil not, neither do they spin: *Matthew 6:28*

Therefore take no thought, saying, What shall we eat? or, What shall we drink? or, Wherewithal shall we be clothed? *Matthew 6:31*

Take therefore no thought for the morrow: for the morrow shall take thought for the things of itself. Sufficient unto the day is the evil thereof. *Matthew 6:34*

MEDITATION

The words of Jesus, here, are meant to help the disciples learn to separate themselves from worldly concerns. He has told them that they will be fishers of men. To do so, they have to be fully committed to listening to Him and let go of concerns. Jesus tells his followers that it makes no sense to worry.

In Matthew 6:27, Jesus says that we cannot increase our stature by worrying. He uses a simple analogy to share the futility of worry.

Worry is not a solution. Worry will not help us accomplish anything. However, worry can hinder us. In fact, doctors and researchers report that stress can cause physical pain, aggravate illnesses and even lead to our deaths.

What worries you?

_____

_____

_____

_____

_____

How has worrying affected your energy level? Your relationships?

_____

_____

_____

_____

_____

_____

Has worry resolved any problems?

_____

_____

_____

MEMORY VERSE

Therefore I say unto you, Take no thought for your life, what ye shall eat, or what ye shall drink; nor yet for your body, what ye shall put on. Is not the life more than meat, and the body than raiment? *Matthew 6:25*

+ Now, spend a few moments praying for freedom from your negative feeling.

Impatient

Intolerant of delay

Restless

Have you the patience of Job? (James 5:11) It is difficult to wait for God to deliver us from a situation, heal our sickness, bless a family member… answer any of our many prayers.

Baptists often say, "God doesn't always come when you want him, but He's right on time!"

Better than anyone else, God can and will deliver. Millions can testify to His goodness! We must remember what He has done for us so far and know that He will deliver us again, in His time.

Wait on the Lord: be of good courage, and he shall strengthen thine heart: wait, I say on the Lord. *Psalm 27:14*

Our soul waiteth for the Lord: he is our help and our shield. For our heart shall rejoice in him, because we have trusted in his holy name. *Psalm 33:20-21*.

But they that wait upon the Lord shall renew their strength; they shall mount up with wings as eagles; they shall run, and not be weary; and they shall walk, and not faint. *Isaiah 40:31*

MEDITATION

Our tests build our character. Our deliverance glorifies the Lord. He is worthy of the praise and His blessings are worth the wait.

Do you recognize how waiting is building your character?

_____

_____

_____

_____

_____

How are you learning to depend on God and be less dependent on the world during this time?

_____

_____

_____

_____

_____

_____

What is your attitude and behavior like as you wait? Are you remaining friendly and positive?

_____

_____

_____

Behold, we count them happy which endure. Ye have heard of the patience of Job, and have seen the end of the Lord that the Lord is very pitiful, and of tender mercy. *James 5:11*

+ Now, spend a few moments praying for freedom from your negative feeling.

Bitter

Cynical

Unpleasant

Full of anguish

Bitter people are usually unpleasant. Their circle of friends, if they have any friends, includes people who are also bitter. The conversations are always laden with gossip and bad news reports. You will notice that they are the ones who always know who has died, who was in an accident, who filed bankruptcy, who was incarcerated and who was laid off.

If someone comes in with good news, the bitter person is the one that mumbles something about the person's character. Pessimism is not a trait of someone who has Jesus on the inside. Jesus says that we are not to hide our light under a bushel but to give light to others (Matthew 5:15).

Happy is that people, that is in such a case: yea, happy is that people, whose God is the Lord. *Psalm 144:15*

With His limitless mercy, God gives us a present each day – the sun has come up! We unwrap a new day that we can try to enjoy. Let go of yesterday!

Therefore if any man be in Christ, he is a new creature: old things are passed away; behold, all things are become new.
2 Corinthians 5:17

And he hath put a new song in my mouth, even praise unto our God: many shall see it, and fear, and shall trust in the Lord.
Psalm 40:3

MEDITATION

Are you holding on to something that happened years ago? Do you spend half of your day concentrating on the bad things that have happened? Do you spend the other half predicting bad things for tomorrow? How many more days are you going to give away to the devil?

_____

_____

_____

_____

_____

God deserves from us new songs. How does holding onto bitterness insult the blessing of a new day?

_____

_____

_____

_____

_____

Even if you don't say it aloud, do you think bad things when someone relates good news? Is this a habit that pleases God?

_____

_____

_____

_____

_____

MEMORY VERSE

Praise ye the Lord. Sing unto the Lord a new song, and his praise in the congregation of saints. *Psalm 149:1*

+ Now, spend a few moments praying for freedom from your negative feeling.

Defeated

Vanquished

Beaten

We will be wounded here on earth. We will lose some battles. However, there is no permanent loss for a Christian. A Christian is never finished off unless he follows in the way of the evil one. Jesus has even conquered death for Christians. So, not even the death of our bodies will end our relationship with the Father. There has been a place prepared for us.

He will swallow up death in victory; and the Lord GOD will wipe away tears from off all faces; and the rebuke of his people shall he take away from off all the earth: for the Lord hath spoken it. *Isaiah 25:8*

But thanks be to God, which giveth us the victory through our Lord Jesus Christ. *1 Corinthians 15:57*

Losses on earth do not matter to someone who knows that having Christ is most important. Losing our relationship with Christ is true defeat.

Yea doubtless, and I count all things but loss for the excellency of the knowledge of Christ Jesus my Lord: for whom I have suffered the loss of all things, and do count them but dung, that I may win Christ. *Philippians 3:8*

The Bible promises victory for believers and delivers on the promises. God saved many from total destruction. The famous stories – Moses was able to part the sea, the three Hebrew boys survived the fiery furnace; Daniel slept soundly in a lion's den and David lived to fight and win numerous battles. These are not the only victories. There are countless other examples in the Bible and in the testimonies of present-day Christian. Even with thousands of tongues each, they could not tell it all.

MEDITATION

Was your loss a battle you fought for a group or organization? Was your loss a personal loss?

_____

_____

_____

_____

_____

Do you believe you made some mistakes?

_____

_____

_____

_____

_____

What victories can you point to in your past to give you strength for this low period?

_____

_____

_____

_____

MEMORY VERSE

For whatsoever is born of God overcometh the world: and this is the victory that overcometh the world, even our faith. *1 John 5:4*

+ Now, spend a few moments praying for freedom from your negative feeling.

Depressed

Sad

Gloomy

Dejected

Luke 24 provides for us a reason that Christians should never be sad. The setting is that Jesus has been crucified and his body has been placed in a sepulcher. But, Jesus was not there. Below, is a verse from the 24th chapter of Luke in which Jesus asks two men why they were sad. The two men do not recognize Jesus at first. Eventually, they and others realize that Jesus still lives!

And he said unto them, What manner of communications are these that ye have one to another, as ye walk, and are sad? *Luke 24:17*

And he said unto them, Why are ye troubled? and why do thoughts arise in your hearts? Behold my hands and my feet, that it is I myself: handle me, and see; for a spirit hath not flesh and bones, as ye see me have. *Luke 24:38-39*

The scriptures remind us to remain joyous because our Savior is alive and has reconciled us with God.

Then he said unto them, Go your way, eat the fat, and drink the sweet, and send portions unto them for whom nothing is prepared: for this day is holy unto our Lord: neither be ye sorry; for the joy of the Lord is your strength. *Nehemiah 8:10*

For if, when we were enemies, we were reconciled to God by the death of his Son, much more, being reconciled, we shall be saved by his life. And not only so, but we also joy in God through our Lord Jesus Christ, by whom we have now received the atonement. *Romans 5:10-11*

MEDITATION

What could be more depressing than hearing your Savior would be killed? He was sent to deliver you. He had spoken about a better place and abundant love for everyone regardless of your status in life!

They tried to kill him but they did not succeed. And guess what? No one can kill your spirit either! Death does not have the power to claim the spirit of a believer.

Write down the events that have cause you to feel depressed.

_____

_____

_____

_____

_____

If your spirit cannot be killed, can you now think more positively about your present condition?

_____

_____

_____

_____

Try concentrating on the fact that Jesus lives inside you. The supreme victor is inside you. How does that make you feel about what you can handle?

_____

_____

_____

_____

_____

M E M O R Y   V E R S E

Restore unto me the joy of thy salvation; and uphold me with thy free spirit. *Psalm 51:12*

+ Now, spend a few moments praying for freedom from your negative feeling.

Discouraged

Hopeless

Lack confidence

You're thinking: what's the use, right? Things are not going to change. It will always be this way. Of course, you know that is not true. But, pitying yourself is comfortable at the moment. Having hope for tomorrow takes more effort. You don't feel like making the effort.

All parties have to come to end – even pity parties. Encourage yourself in the Word.

And David was greatly distressed; for the people spake of stoning him, because the soul of all the people was grieved, every man for his sons and for his daughters: but David encouraged himself in the Lord his God. *1 Samuel 30:6*

Be strong and of a good courage, fear not, nor be afraid of them: for the Lord thy God, he it is that doth go with thee; he will not fail thee, nor forsake thee. *Deuteronomy 31:6*

Be of good courage, and he shall strengthen your heart, all ye that hope in the Lord. *Psalm 31:24*

MEDITATION

You just read that the warrior David was distressed but he encouraged himself in the Lord. David's city had been destroyed. His wives had been taken captive. Everyone had cried until they were too tired to weep. Are you now, at that point? Or have you still some tears to shed before ending your pity party?

_____

_____

_____

_____

The Bible says that after encouraging himself, David asked the priest to bring him his ephod (battle gear). Then, he asked the Lord if he should pursue the enemy. He also asked if he would win.

Knowing this, can you brush yourself off and reset for the challenges in your life?

God told David to pursue. He also told him that he would win and recover all. David won an immediate victory. It may not be immediate but you will also enjoy victories.

Remaining hopeful puts you in the pathway of a blessing. Faith is believing. Hope is expecting. The Lord can work when He finds those ingredients in us. What are you made of?

_____

_____

_____

_____

MEMORY VERSE

Now the God of hope fill you with all joy and peace in believing, that ye may abound in hope, through the power of the Holy Ghost. *Romans 15:13*

+ Now, spend a few moments praying for freedom from your negative feeling.

Lost

No longer belonging to God

Without purpose

The 15th chapter of Luke provides us with three parables: the parable of the lost sheep; the parable of the lost coin; and the parable of the lost son. With each story, Jesus declares that people are always happy when the lost is found.

Lost sheep
What man of you, having an hundred sheep, if he lose one of them, doth not leave the ninety and nine in the wilderness, and go after that which is lost, until he find it? *Luke 15:4*

And when he cometh home, he calleth together his friends and neighbours, saying unto them, Rejoice with me; for I have found my sheep which was lost. *Luke 15:6*

Lost coin
Either what woman having ten pieces of silver, if she lose one piece, doth not light a candle, and sweep the house, and seek diligently till she find it? *Luke 15:8*

And when she hath found it, she calleth her friends and her neighbours together, saying, Rejoice with me; for I have found the piece which I had lost. *Luke 15:9*

Lost son

For this my son was dead, and is alive again; he was lost, and is found. And they began to be merry. *Luke 15:24*

And when he cometh home, he calleth together his friends and neighbours, saying unto them, Rejoice with me; for I have found my sheep which was lost. *Luke 15:6*

Jesus says that Heaven celebrates when a soul is won or reclaimed for the Kingdom.

I say unto you, that likewise joy shall be in heaven over one sinner that repenteth, more than over ninety and nine just persons, which need no repentance. *Luke 15:7*

Likewise, I say unto you, there is joy in the presence of the angels of God over one sinner that repenteth. *Luke 15:10*

MEDITATION

Jesus gives three examples of the good feeling people have when that which is lost is returned. He goes further to say that there is jubilation in Heaven when a sinner repents. How does it make you feel to know that Heaven will rejoice if you repent and join/rejoin the flock?

_____

_____

_____

_____

_____

As was mentioned in the Introduction, Jesus is the shepherd and we are the sheep. He holds himself responsible for us. In John 10:16, Jesus says he will make one fold. He is interested in those sheep that are following and those who are not following. Jesus declares that He will give his life for the sheep.

How does it feel to know that Jesus does not give up on lost sheep?

_____

_____

_____

_____

_____

_____

Jesus asked the disciples to seek the lost. With the Great Commission, Jesus asks them to teach and baptize all nations (Matthew 28:19). The duty of today's disciples is to carry on the commandment.

God is waiting to receive you. Good churches are waiting to receive you. You don't have to feel lost anymore. Write Luke 5:32 below:

_____

_____

_____

_____

_____

MEMORY VERSE

For the Son of man is come to seek and to save that which was lost. *Luke 19:10*

+ Now, spend a few moments praying for freedom from your negative feeling.

Tempted

Attracted to sin

Enticed to do wrong

The Bible tells us in the 6th chapter of 1 Corinthians that our bodies are members of Christ. Our bodies are temples. The 20th chapter of Exodus provides the Ten Commandments for us. There are directives throughout the Bible.

What tempts you may not tempt someone else. What entices someone else may not even turn your head. Unholy contact with the opposite or same sex is an easy sin for us to identify. Married people love to point fingers at single people.

But sin is sin. James writes in the 12th verse of the 2nd chapter: For whosoever shall keep the whole law, and yet offend in one point, he is guilty of all.

We can destroy our temple by overindulging in food and drink. We can use our words and actions to hurt others. We can choose vanity over compassion. We can choose materialism over love. We can be dishonest and insincere. We can refuse to repent.

Resisting temptation is not easy. All have sinned, and come short of the glory of God *(Romans 3:23).*

Jesus says we have to stay alert and ask for help.

Watch and pray, that ye enter not into temptation: the spirit indeed is willing, but the flesh is weak. *Matthew 26:41*

And lead us not into temptation, but deliver us from evil: For thine is the kingdom, and the power, and the glory, for ever. Amen. *Matthew 6:13*

It is the power of the Lord that helps us to resist temptation. We cannot do it alone.

There hath no temptation taken you but such as is common to man: but God is faithful, who will not suffer you to be tempted above that ye are able; but will with the temptation also make a way to escape, that ye may be able to bear it. *1 Corinthians 10:13*

MEDITATION

Some of your temptations are easier to avoid than others. Can you identify the ones that you can conquer right away?

_____

_____

_____

_____

_____

What temptations require more help from God? Write them below and begin a conversation with the Lord. He knows about them anyway. But, He'd like to hear from you.

_____

_____

_____

_____

Blessed is the man that endureth temptation: for when he is tried, he shall receive the crown of life, which the Lord hath promised to them that love him *(James 1:12)*

+ Now, spend a few moments praying for freedom from your negative feeling.

Betrayed

Sadness due to another's deception

Distress after being delivered to the enemy

Are you feeling the sadness of betrayal? Has someone wronged you? Told your secrets? Caused you problems with a loved one or your employer?

Jesus knew beforehand that he would be betrayed. He knew what to expect.

Behold, we go up to Jerusalem; and the Son of man shall be betrayed unto the chief priests and unto the scribes, and they shall condemn him to death, *Matthew 20:18*

Are you better than Christ? We should expect for the world to be mean to us sometimes.

If ye were of the world, the world would love his own: but because ye are not of the world, but I have chosen you out of the world, therefore the world hateth you. *John 15:19*

Hear the word of the Lord, ye that tremble at his word; Your brethren that hated you, that cast you out for my name's sake, said, Let the Lord be glorified: but he shall appear to your joy, and they shall be ashamed. *Isaiah 66:5*

We know that His betrayal led to the crucifixion. But, we must not forget that the crucifixion led to His resurrection. All of which led to His victory over death and our salvation. That means we have final victory over Satan.

Yes, you have been betrayed. Your feelings are appropriate but you will need to start believing for your victory. The Bible promises double for your trouble.

For your shame ye shall have double; and for confusion they shall rejoice in their portion: therefore in their land they shall possess the double: everlasting joy shall be unto them. *Isaiah 61:7*

MEDITATION

Express your feelings about being betrayed.

_____

_____

_____

_____

_____

Jesus knew that he would be betrayed by Judas and denied by Peter. But, he still treated them well. What do you think about that?

_____

_____

_____

_____

_____

How does it make you feel to know that Jesus was betrayed but received ultimate victory?

_____

_____

_____

_____

Bad things sometimes need to happen for dramatic glory. How does it feel to know that Jesus' betrayal was necessary for his death and necessary for your salvation? Do you think your betrayal can eventually be linked to God's glory?

_____

_____

_____

_____

_____

MEMORY VERSE

The Lord said unto my Lord (God to Christ), Sit thou at my right hand, until I make thine enemies thy footstool. *Psalm 110:1*

+ Now, spend a few moments praying for freedom from your negative feeling.

Lonely

Saddened by the absence of company

Feeling all alone

We all can feel lonely at times. External causes such as a break-up, divorce or death can lead to feelings of loneliness. Or, it may be internal forces such as your decision to give up a habit or participate with a different organization. Whether external or internal, these are changes that can affect your social life.

But God, the Father, the Son and the Holy Ghost are with you everywhere you go. So, you really are never ever alone.

Teaching them to observe all things whatsoever I have commanded you: and, lo, I am with you alway, even unto the end of the world. Amen. *Matthew 28:20*

And, behold, I am with thee, and will keep thee in all places whither thou goest, and will bring thee again into this land; for I will not leave thee, until I have done that which I have spoken to thee of. *Genesis 28:14*

And his master saw that the Lord was with him, and that the Lord made all that he did to prosper in his hand. Genesis 39:3

The keeper of the prison looked not to any thing that was under his hand; because the Lord was with him, and that which he did, the Lord made it to prosper. *Genesis 39:23*

And David behaved himself wisely in all his ways; and the Lord was with him. *1 Samuel 18:14*

And Samuel grew, and the Lord was with him, and did let none of his words fall to the ground. *1 Samuel 3:19*

I am Alpha and Omega, the beginning and the end, the first and the last *Revelation 22:13*

MEDITATION

What has triggered your feelings of loneliness?

_____

_____

_____

_____

_____

_____

In the cited verses, you see God was with Joseph as he served his master, Potiphar. He was also with Joseph in prison.

God is with us during our highs and our lows. How does it make you feel that God never leaves us alone?

_____

_____

_____

_____

_____

Revelations 22:13 tells us God is always present. Wherever you are, God is there. Wherever you are not, God is there also. How does it feel to know that God is here with you now as you are meditating on his Word?

_____

_____

_____

_____

_____

MEMORY VERSE

At that day ye shall know that I am in my Father, and ye in me, and I in you. *John 14:20*

+ Now, spend a few moments praying for freedom from your negative feeling.

Weary

Mentally or physically exhausted

Tired

We are busy people. It takes a great deal of energy to conduct our lives. We will become exhausted and sometimes we will want to give up. But, what we actually need to do is pray and rest. Ask God for a good night's sleep and energy to keep working.

And on the seventh day God ended his work which he had made; and he rested on the seventh day from all his work which he had made. *Genesis 2:2*

And he said, My presence shall go with thee, and I will give thee rest. *Exodus 33:14*

The Bible says that we should not give in to our exhaustion or the frustration of our work. We must carry on, to carry out the assignments He has for us.

But they that wait upon the Lord shall renew their strength; they shall mount up with wings as eagles; they shall run, and not be weary; and they shall walk, and not faint. *Isaiah 40:31*

But ye, brethren, be not weary in well doing. *2 Thessalonians 3:13*

MEDITATION

What has made you tired?

_____

_____

_____

_____

_____

_____

Let this sink in: If you keep on going, you will get there. Why does that
sound too simple?

_____

_____

_____

_____

_____

_____

God says that He is able to give you rest. He says he is your strength. How
can you remind yourself that God is running this race with you?

_____

_____

_____

And let us not be weary in well doing: for in due season we shall reap, if we faint not. *Galatians 6:9*

+ Now, spend a few moments praying for freedom from your negative feeling.

Vengeful

Desiring to seek vengeance

Vindictive

There will be ways that God will allow for you to play a hand in serving justice. For example, you may have to sue someone. You may have to testify at a hearing. God will open those avenues if they are in His will.

The point to remember is that God will create a means to justly handle your enemy. You must be prayerful and stay out of it unless God shows you a role. Sometimes, the consequence for your enemy will not be immediate or public. Sometimes, it will not require your participation.

And don't forget, you've made mistakes as well. You may have hurt someone and God may have shown you mercy.

To me belongeth vengeance, and recompence; their foot shall slide in due time: for the day of their calamity is at hand, and the things that shall come upon them make haste. *Deuteronomy 32:35*

O Lord God, to whom vengeance belongeth; O God, to whom vengeance belongeth, shew thyself. *Psalm 94:1*

God is jealous, and the Lord revengeth; the Lord revengeth, and is furious; the Lord will take vengeance on his adversaries, and he reserveth wrath for his enemies. *Nahum 1:2*

Say not thou, I will recompense evil; but wait on the Lord, and he shall save thee. *Proverbs 20:22*

MEDITATION

Why are scenes of revenge playing in your head?

_____

_____

_____

_____

_____

How could seeking revenge worsen your situation?

_____

_____

_____

_____

_____

How could seeking revenge anger the Lord?

_____

_____

_____

_____

_____

_____

So, now, what's the plan?

_____

_____

_____

_____

_____

MEMORY VERSE

Dearly beloved, avenge not yourselves, but rather give place unto wrath: for it is written, Vengeance is mine; I will repay, saith the Lord. *Romans 12:19*

+ Now, spend a few moments praying for freedom from your negative feeling.

Hate

Dislike intensely

Loathe

Despise

Hate can cause judgment for you. There is nothing worse than God's anger.

And when the Lord saw that Leah was hated, he opened her womb: but Rachel was barren. *Genesis 29:31*

But if any man hate his neighbour, and lie in wait for him, and rise up against him, and smite him mortally that he die, and fleeth into one of these cities: Then the elders of his city shall send and fetch him thence, and deliver him into the hand of the avenger of blood, that he may die. *Deuteronomy 19:11-12*

**If any man take a wife, and go in unto her, and hate her.....
the elders of that city shall take that man and chastise him;**
Deuteronomy 22:13, 18

Thou shalt not hate thy brother in thine heart: thou shalt in any wise rebuke thy neighbour, and not suffer sin upon him.
Leviticus 19:17

Love is so important to God that Jesus made a mandate.

A new commandment I give unto you, That ye love one another; as I have loved you, that ye also love one another. *John 13:34*

MEDITATION

What has caused you to have hate for others?

_____

_____

_____

_____

_____

Read this verse:

**And we have known and believed the love that God hath to us.
God is love; and he that dwelleth in love dwelleth in God, and
God in him.** *1 John 4:16*

How is harboring hate disrupting your relationship with God?

_____

_____

_____

_____

_____

We read in the previous pages that hate can bring harm to us. Jesus also
says that we should pray for and be pleasant to those who hate us.

**But I say unto you, Love your enemies, bless them that curse
you, do good to them that hate you, and pray for them which
despitefully use you, and persecute you;** *Matthew 5:44*

Although you may feel that you should be able to hate your enemies,
understand that it works both ways. Your enemies hinder themselves by
hating you. How can you use that fact to move forward?

_____

_____

_____

_____

MEMORY VERSE

He that loveth not knoweth not God; for God is love. *I John 4:8*

+ Now, spend a few moments praying for freedom from your negative feeling.

Disappointed

Concentrating on failure

Thwarted expectations

When things do not work out as you planned, God may be up to something. He says His ways are not our ways. (Isaiah 55:8). Your plan may not have been the best plan to bring Him glorify.

Be strong and of a good courage, fear not, nor be afraid of them: for the Lord thy God, he it is that doth go with thee; he will not fail thee, nor forsake thee. *Deuteronomy 31:6*

My flesh and my heart faileth: but God is the strength of my heart, and my portion for ever. *Psalm 73:26*

Fight the good fight of faith, lay hold on eternal life, whereunto thou art also called, and hast professed a good profession before many witnesses. *I Timothy 6:12*

Stay prayerful as the barren Hannah. She was barren for several years but remained faithful. She gave birth to an important leader. What if what God has for you is even better than you expected?!

And she said, Oh my lord, as thy soul liveth, my lord, I am the woman that stood by thee here, praying unto the Lord. For this child I prayed; and the Lord hath given me my petition which I asked of him: *I Samuel 1*

MEDITATION

Why are you disappointed?

_____

_____

_____

_____

_____

_____

What have you learned from this disappointment?

_____

_____

_____

_____

_____

God says He won't fail. God has been known to give His children more
than they could ask or think. How does that make you feel?

_____

_____

_____

_____

_____

And we know that all things work together for good to them that love God, to them who are the called according to his purpose. *Romans 8:28*

+ Now, spend a few moments praying for freedom from your negative feeling.

Angry

Furious

Resentful

Wrathful

Getting angry is human and even divine. God gets angry. Jesus took offense to some things. But, staying angry is not healthy and not conducive to the Christian lifestyle.

Although your blood may be boiling for good reason, you must turn your energy toward cooling it. Communicate to others in a balanced tone and with controlled actions. Doing the opposite may cause problems for you. You'll want to avoid the consequences of emotional behavior.

He that is slow to wrath is of great understanding: but he that is hasty of spirit exalteth folly. *Proverbs 14:29*

A soft answer turneth away wrath: but grievous words stir up anger. *Proverbs 15:1*

A man of great wrath shall suffer punishment: for if thou deliver him, yet thou must do it again. *Proverbs 19:19*

Be ye angry, and sin not: let not the sun go down upon your wrath: *Ephesians 4:26*

MEDITATION

What has set your temperature on high?

_____

_____

_____

_____

_____

It is definitely better to release emotion then to hold on to them. However, there are appropriate ways to release anger. How do you plan to release your anger?

_____

_____

_____

_____

_____

What things bring you comfort when you are emotional?

_____

_____

_____

_____

_____

Be not hasty in thy spirit to be angry: for anger resteth in the bosom of fools. *Ecclesiastes 7:9*

+ Now, spend a few moments praying for freedom from your negative feeling.

Envy

Jealous

Coveting what belongs to another

Discontent with one's own status, image, possessions

We cannot be the kind of people that bad-mouth our co-workers or neighbors when they purchase a new car or install a pool. We also cannot be the kind of people who are copycats. Pray and work for necessities and luxuries. Give God thanks for all that you receive. Always be content.

Let us not be desirous of vain glory, provoking one another, envying one another. *Galatians 5:26*

For where envying and strife is, there is confusion and every evil work. *James 3:16*

Sometimes, we are jealous of those who are in charge because they are able to complicate our lives. Or, we are jealous of people who seem to get away with wrong doing. But, the Bible says don't do that.

Envy thou not the oppressor, and choose none of his ways. *Proverbs 3:31*

Let not thine heart envy sinners: but be thou in the fear of the Lord all the day long. *Proverbs 23:17*

Fret not thyself because of evildoers, neither be thou envious against the workers of iniquity. *Psalm 37:1*

Be not thou envious against evil men, neither desire to be with them. *Proverbs 24:1*

Fret not thyself because of evil men, neither be thou envious at the wicked; *Proverbs 24:19*

MEDITATION

Why are you envious of others?

_____

_____

_____

_____

_____

Is there a natural or supernatural way to obtain this "thing" you want?

_____

_____

_____

_____

_____

Are you being careful not to show displeasure to God for giving you what you need? Can this "thing" you want bring glory to God?

_____

_____

_____

But seek ye first the kingdom of God, and his righteousness; and all these things shall be added unto you. *Matthew 6:33*

+ Now, spend a few moments praying for freedom from your negative feeling.

Superior

Exalted

Snobby

Haughty

Calm down Mr. and Mrs. Wonderful. The only One who is Superior is God. A Christian does not look down on others whom you think do not measure up to you internally, externally, financially, socially, or even spiritually.

God does not need church folk. He needs Christians. There is a difference. It is amazing how we pass judgment while sitting in the Lord's house. Remarkable nerve!

Jesus paid the price but none of our birth certificates came with a "Get into Heaven Free" card. We didn't receive one when we got baptized and no one passes them out to us when we turn 65. Better get a grip before God does.

And the afflicted people thou wilt save: but thine eyes are upon the haughty, that thou mayest bring them down. *2 Samuel 22:28*

Moreover the Lord saith, Because the daughters of Zion are haughty, and walk with stretched forth necks and wanton eyes, walking and mincing as they go, and making a tinkling with their feet: Therefore the Lord will smite with a scab the crown of the head of the daughters of Zion...*Isaiah 3:16-17*

Behold, the Lord, the Lord of hosts, shall lop the bough with terror: and the high ones of stature shall be hewn down, and the haughty shall be humbled. *Isaiah 10:33*

Pride goeth before destruction, and an haughty spirit before a fall. Better it is to be of an humble spirit with the lowly, than to divide the spoil with the proud. *Proverbs 16:18-19*

The earth mourneth and fadeth away, the world languisheth and fadeth away, the haughty people of the earth do languish. *Isaiah 24:4*

And they were haughty, and committed abomination before me: therefore I took them away as I saw good. *Ezekiel 16:50*

MEDITATION

God gives His children grace and mercy daily. Some of His children were born with more visible attributes than others. Why do you think you are better than other people?

_____

_____

_____

_____

It is a fact that God has blessed some with more beauty; more talent; more strength; more intelligence or more prosperity than others. Is it because He loves them more?

_____

_____

_____

_____

I think it is a test. What do you think about Luke 12:48 (to whom much is given, much is required)?

_____

_____

_____

_____

_____

MEMORY VERSE

For I say, through the grace given unto me, to every man that is among you, not to think of himself more highly than he ought to think; but to think soberly, according as God hath dealt to every man the measure of faith. *Romans 12:3*

+ Now, spend a few moments praying for freedom from your negative feeling.

Unloved/Scorned

Disliked

Hated

Despised

Nobody loves me. That feeling arises in single people, married people, people in small families and people in large families. It is an empty feeling – a feeling of being emotionally malnourished. However, it is a needless feeling, rooted in a lie. God loves us. Find your nourishment in the Word.

Nor height, nor depth, nor any other creature, shall be able to separate us from the love of God, which is in Christ Jesus our Lord. *Romans 8:39*

If you are being actively scorned, take comfort in what Jesus says.

And ye shall be hated of all men for my name's sake: but he that endureth to the end shall be saved. *Matthew 10:22*

If the world hate you, ye know that it hated me before it hated you. *John 15:18*

I have given them thy word; and the world hath hated them, because they are not of the world, even as I am not of the world. *John 17:14*

If you feel unloved and hated, show God even more dedication to Him. He will reward your love and devotion more than any person on earth.

For God is not unrighteous to forget your work and labour of love, which ye have shewed toward his name, in that ye have ministered to the saints, and do minister. *Hebrews 6:10*

But whoso keepeth his word, in him verily is the love of God perfected: hereby know we that we are in him. *1 John 2:5*

MEDITATION

Why do you feel that no one loves you?

_____

_____

_____

_____

_____

What proof do you have that God loves you?

_____

_____

_____

_____

_____

What can you do to deepen your relationship with God to reap a feeling of deeper love from Him?

_____

_____

_____

_____

_____

MEMORY VERSE

For God so loved the world, that he gave his only begotten Son, that whosoever believeth in him should not perish, but have everlasting life. *John 3:16*

+ Now, spend a few moments praying for freedom from your negative feeling.

Unlovable/Unattractive

Ugly

Unacceptable

We are not too nerdy, too fat, too skinny, too dark-skinned, or too goofy for God. You hair isn't too thin or too short. You don't have too many moles or too many pimples. God is not bothered by your stretch marks or your calluses. God is sharp enough to know that, sometimes, beauty is only skin deep.

And the Lord said unto him, Now do ye Pharisees make clean the outside of the cup and the platter; but your inward part is full of ravening and wickedness. *Luke 11:39*

While our beauty is subjectively judged on the basis of our proportions, God uses a different scale. God looks at our hearts. All of us have the propensity to be lovely to Him because we all have the option to love him with all of our heart. God is moved by our faithfulness.

For the eyes of the Lord run to and fro throughout the whole earth, to shew himself strong in the behalf of them whose heart is perfect toward him. Herein thou hast done foolishly: therefore from henceforth thou shalt have wars. *2 Chronicles 16:9*

Ensure that your insides are beautiful.

That he would grant you, according to the riches of his glory, to be strengthened with might by his Spirit in the inner man. *Ephesians 3:16*

Favour is deceitful, and beauty is vain: but a woman that feareth the Lord, she shall be praised. *Proverbs 31:30*

Everyone has a purpose and the purpose is not based on the world's standards but God's agenda.

Before I formed thee in the belly I knew thee; and before thou camest forth out of the womb I sanctified thee, and I ordained thee a prophet unto the nations. *Jeremiah 1:5*

MEDITATION

Everyone you meet is not "beautiful." Everyone who is on TV is not "beautiful." But, everyone has the potential for value beyond their physical appearance. What is causing you to devalue yourself?

_____

_____

_____

_____

_____

Your body is a temple. There are things you can do to respect the body/ temple God gave you to live in. Good hygiene, good nutrition and exercise will provide us with a measure of strength and health. In what ways are prioritizing your temple?

_____

_____

_____

_____

_____

As we become caught up in our appearance, we forget to feed ourselves with the bread of life. When we are filled up with God on the inside, others will see the beauty of the Lord. Give examples of when you have fallen for someone's heart despite their imperfections?

_____

_____

_____

_____

_____

MEMORY VERSE

But the Lord said unto Samuel, Look not on his countenance, or on the height of his stature; because I have refused him: for the Lord seeth not as man seeth; for man looketh on the outward appearance, but the Lord looketh on the heart. *1 Samuel 16:7*

+ Now, spend a few moments praying for freedom from your negative feeling.

Neglected

Not cared for

Unattended

Have those in your life become too busy to care for you? God can hold you. He is listening when they are not. He is always interested in you even when the world seems to be content with ignoring you.

Jesus specializes in helping the ones who are forgotten. In the 8th chapter of Matthew, a leper worshipped Jesus and asked the Lord to make him clean.

And Jesus put forth his hand, and touched him, saying, I will; be thou clean. And immediately his leprosy was cleansed. *Matthew 8:3*

All you need to do is call on the name of Jesus!

And he will love thee, and bless thee, and multiply thee: he will also bless the fruit of thy womb, and the fruit of thy land, thy corn, and thy wine, and thine oil, the increase of thy kine, and the flocks of thy sheep, in the land which he sware unto thy fathers to give thee. *Deuteronomy 7:13*

Blessed are the poor in spirit: for theirs is the kingdom of heaven. *Matthew 5:3*

And I will pray the Father, and he shall give you another Comforter, that he may abide with you for ever; *John 14:16*

MEDITATION

Why do you feel neglected?

_____

_____

_____

_____

_____

You are not unattended. You have the love and comfort of God, the Father, the Son and Holy Spirit. What promises has God made to provide for you?

_____

_____

_____

_____

_____

Do you understand that you have the power to eradicate this feeling by calling on Jesus? How can you feel closer to the Lord?

_____

_____

_____

_____

_____

_____

Casting all your care upon him; for he careth for you.
1 Peter 5:7

+ Now, spend a few moments praying for freedom from your negative feeling.

Sorrowful/Bereaved

Saddened by loss

Grieved

Heartbroken

Oh, what can mend a broken heart? So many songwriters, both secular and spiritual, have dealt with the subject of healing broken hearts.

The only way is to open your bruised and wounded heart to love. You may choose another human to love but if he or she was not first chosen by God, you could be in for another heart break.

The best way to heal is to love God more intensely. I watched my grandmother survive 20-plus years after losing my grandfather. Wed as a teenager, she had been married nearly 50 years when he passed. Statistics show that long-time partners die within a year or two of the other because they miss the other partner so much. But, my grandmother immersed herself in reading the Bible. She found closeness in her relationship with God.

The Lord is nigh unto them that are of a broken heart; and saveth such as be of a contrite spirit. *Psalm 34:18*

He healeth the broken in heart, and bindeth up their wounds. *Psalm 147:3*

And it shall come to pass in the day that the Lord shall give thee rest from thy sorrow, and from thy fear, and from the hard bondage wherein thou wast made to serve, *Isaiah 14:3*

And ye now therefore have sorrow: but I will see you again, and your heart shall rejoice, and your joy no man taketh from you. *John 16:22*

MEDITATION

What has caused your sadness?

_____

_____

_____

_____

_____

_____

Loved ones cannot be replaced. Others can come along and you may love them in a different way. I know a lady who lost her husband but has decided to volunteer with children. In what ways can you actively seek relationships with others?

_____

_____

_____

_____

_____

_____

Create a plan ahead of time about how you will spend the holidays and other special dates that you once shared with your loved one.

_____

_____

_____

_____

_____

We can usually fill up our days. But late afternoon and evening can sometimes be the loneliest times when we are grieving loss. Take the time to pray, read the Bible, write in a journal. If nothing is helping, talk with the Lord about seeing a doctor. Depression is a serious illness and you should not be ashamed to ask for temporary help.

MEMORY VERSE

And God shall wipe away all tears from their eyes; and there shall be no more death, neither sorrow, nor crying, neither shall there be any more pain: for the former things are passed away. *Revelation 21:4*

+ Now, spend a few moments praying for freedom from your negative feeling.

Prideful

Cherishing self

Overly impressed with self

Sometimes, we think we can get along without God. We can figure it out. The truth is we are not smarter or stronger than God.

None of us have made it this far without the Lord. One of the problems we have in society is that people are forgetting or refusing to give credit to the Lord for His blessings. This practice gives rise to a society of people who are self-absorbed.

Christian principles are replaced by the rules of capitalism. The mode of the day is survival of the fittest and not serving the present age.

However, the Bible speaks against human pride. This is truly a dangerous sin. Jesus even calls it evil in Matthew 7:22.

Human pride displaces reverence for God.

For all that is in the world, the lust of the flesh, and the lust of the eyes, and the pride of life, is not of the Father, but is of the world. *1 John 2:16*

The fear of the Lord is to hate evil: pride, and arrogancy, and the evil way, and the froward (disobedient) mouth, do I hate. *Proverbs 8:13*

When pride cometh, then cometh shame: but with the lowly is wisdom. *Proverbs 11:2*

A man's pride shall bring him low: but honour shall uphold the humble in spirit. *Proverbs 29:23*

Nevertheless among the chief rulers also many believed on him; but because of the Pharisees they did not confess him, lest they should be put out of the synagogue: For they loved the praise of men more than the praise of God. *John 12:42-43*

MEDITATION

God starts us off each morning. Humans do not even have the power to wake themselves! God is the true power in our lives. In what ways are you going to change your thoughts about self?

_____

_____

_____

_____

_____

It is He who created us. He is God whether we exist or not. List below the things you really control.

_____

_____

_____

_____

_____

How dangerous is it to be prideful?

_____

_____

_____

_____

_____

MEMORY VERSE

Not a novice, lest being lifted up with pride he fall into the condemnation of the devil. *1 Timothy 3:6*

+ Now, spend a few moments praying for freedom from your negative feeling.

Ruined

Unable to be forgiven

Unable to go on

Destroyed morally, financially, socially, etc.

God's storeroom of second chances is overflowing with grace and mercy. Peter asked Jesus (Matthew 18:21) how many times should he forgive a brother. Jesus said seventy times seven.

Not only does God promise to forgive us, He also has shown us that he can work with a remnant. All we may have left is a thimble of faith. That's enough! A marriage, a situation, a dream may have only a shred of a chance. That's enough! Hallelujah! A shred can be enough.

Else if ye do in any wise go back, and cleave unto the remnant of these nations, even these that remain among you, and shall make marriages with them, and go in unto them, and they to you: *Joshua 23:12*

It may be the Lord thy God will hear all the words of Rabshakeh, whom the king of Assyria his master hath sent to reproach the living God; and will reprove the words which the Lord thy God hath heard: wherefore lift up thy prayer for the remnant that are left. *2 Kings 19:4*

For out of Jerusalem shall go forth a remnant, and they that escape out of mount Zion: the zeal of the Lord of hosts shall do this. *2 Kings 19:31*

Hate the evil, and love the good, and establish judgment in the gate: it may be that the Lord God of hosts will be gracious unto the remnant of Joseph. *Amos 5:15*

MEDITATION

What is your set back?

_____

_____

_____

_____

_____

Why do you think you cannot make a comeback?

_____

_____

_____

_____

_____

God can place a comma where man tries to place a period. Your ending is up to the Lord. How can you do to put yourself in the pathway of God?

_____

_____

_____

_____

And Jesus said unto them, Because of your unbelief: for verily I say unto you, If ye have faith as a grain of mustard seed, ye shall say unto this mountain, Remove hence to yonder place; and it shall remove; and nothing shall be impossible unto you. *Matthew 17:20*

+ Now, spend a few moments praying for freedom from your negative feeling.

Unqualified

Unprepared

Not fit

Some of us feel that we are not ready for the service that God has called us to fulfill.

You know Moses said the same thing. In Exodus, when God called Moses, he had a bunch of excuses.

And Moses said unto the Lord, O my Lord, I am not eloquent, neither heretofore, nor since thou hast spoken unto thy servant: but I am slow of speech, and of a slow tongue. *Exodus 4:10*

But, God promised to be there with him.

Now therefore go, and I will be with thy mouth, and teach thee what thou shalt say. *Exodus 4:12*

When God called Jeremiah, he said he was too young.

Then said I, Ah, Lord GOD! behold, I cannot speak: for I am a child. *Jeremiah 1:6*

God said he saw more in Jeremiah.

But the Lord said unto me, Say not, I am a child: for thou shalt go to all that I shall send thee, and whatsoever I command thee thou shalt speak. Be not afraid of their faces: for I am with thee

to deliver thee, saith the Lord. Then the Lord put forth his hand, and touched my mouth. And the Lord said unto me, Behold, I have put my words in thy mouth. See, I have this day set thee over the nations and over the kingdoms, to root out, and to pull down, and to destroy, and to throw down, to build, and to plant. *Jeremiah 1:7-10*

If God blesses you with a job, opportunity or an assignment, take it. He won't let you fail.

God having provided some better thing for us, that they without us should not be made perfect. *Hebrews 11:40*

And he said unto me, My grace is sufficient for thee: for my strength is made perfect in weakness. Most gladly therefore will I rather glory in my infirmities, that the power of Christ may rest upon me. *2 Corinthians 12:9*

MEDITATION

Why do you feel unprepared?

_____

_____

_____

_____

_____

It is all right to ask the Lord to help you believe. God loves for us to call upon Him. What can you do to become more confident about the task?

_____

_____

_____

Sometimes, it is helpful to remind yourself of past victories and previous blessings. Write down what God has done for you that you did not expect.

_____

_____

_____

_____

_____

MEMORY VERSE

But my God shall supply all your need according to his riches in glory by Christ Jesus. *Philippians 4:19*

+ Now, spend a few moments praying for freedom from your negative feeling.

Guilty

Conscious of wrongdoing

Out of the will of God

God created a process for forgiveness. We must repent with sincere hearts. However, depending on the circumstance, you may owe others an apology.

Although man may recount your sin, Christians are taught that God forgets them.

And they shall teach no more every man his neighbour, and every man his brother, saying, Know the Lord: for they shall all know me, from the least of them unto the greatest of them, saith the Lord: for I will forgive their iniquity, and I will remember their sin no more. *Jeremiah 31:34*

In whom we have redemption through his blood, the forgiveness of sins, according to the riches of his grace; *Ephesians 1:7*

And be ye kind one to another, tenderhearted, forgiving one another, even as God for Christ's sake hath forgiven you. *Ephesians 4:32*

And you, being dead in your sins and the uncircumcision of your flesh, hath he quickened together with him, having forgiven you all trespasses; *Colossians 2:13*

And the prayer of faith shall save the sick, and the Lord shall raise him up; and if he have committed sins, they shall be forgiven him. *James 5:15*

I write unto you, little children, because your sins are forgiven you for his name's sake. *1 John 2:12*

There is no need to feel guilty. All sins are forgivable except one.

And whosoever speaketh a word against the Son of man, it shall be forgiven him: but whosoever speaketh against the Holy Ghost, it shall not be forgiven him, neither in this world, neither in the world to come. *Matthew 12:32*

MEDITATION

Why do you feel guilty? Are you afraid to go to certain places?

_____

_____

_____

_____

_____

_____

_____

In what ways have these verse brought you comfort?

_____

_____

_____

_____

_____

_____

How can you plan to step out in faith and believe that you are forgiven by the Lord?

_____

_____

_____

_____

_____

Saying, Blessed are they whose iniquities are forgiven, and whose sins are covered. *Romans 4:7*

+ Now, spend a few moments praying for freedom from your negative feeling.

Vulnerable

Unprotected

Unsafe

Open to assault

Although you may feel that you are out in the open, there is an invisible shield around you. If you believe in God, then you know that nothing happens to us that God does not allow.

The Lord can take care of you even in the midst of your enemies.

The Lord is my shepherd; I shall not want. He maketh me to lie down in green pastures: he leadeth me beside the still waters. He restoreth my soul: he leadeth me in the paths of righteousness for his name's sake. Yea, though I walk through the valley of the shadow of death, I will fear no evil: for thou art with me; thy rod and thy staff they comfort me. Thou preparest a table before me in the presence of mine enemies: thou anointest my head with oil; my cup runneth over. Surely goodness and mercy shall follow me all the days of my life: and I will dwell in the house of the Lord for ever. *Psalm 23*

Abide thou with me, fear not: for he that seeketh my life seeketh thy life: but with me thou shalt be in safeguard. *1 Samuel 22:23*

Their houses are safe from fear, neither is the rod of God upon them. *Job 21:9*

The name of the Lord is a strong tower: the righteous runneth into it, and is safe. *Proverbs 18:10*

He will not suffer thy foot to be moved: he that keepeth thee will not slumber. *Psalm 121:3*

The God of my rock; in him will I trust: he is my shield, and the horn of my salvation, my high tower, and my refuge, my saviour; thou savest me from violence. *2 Samuel 22:3*

MEDITATION

Why do you feel vulnerable?

_____

_____

_____

_____

_____

It is all right to ask the Lord to "hide you" when you feel uncomfortable. God loves to hear from us. What can you say to God?

_____

_____

_____

_____

_____

_____

What can you do each day to remind yourself that God is with you?

_____

_____

_____

_____

_____

MEMORY   VERSE

And he said, The Lord is my rock, and my fortress, and my deliverer; *2 Samuel 22:2*

+ Now, spend a few moments praying for freedom from your negative feeling.

Greedy

Strongly desirous of wealth, profit

Overly interested in gain

Materialism and vanity have gotten out of control since the creation of credit cards and other luxuries, such as plastic surgery. We have to be careful not to become slaves of greed.

Jesus died so that we could have life more abundantly but there are lines that we must not cross. He was speaking more of the fact that we have the opportunity to have life on earth and then transition to another realm in Heaven. We must be careful not to strive for Heaven on earth.

Yea, they are greedy dogs which can never have enough, and they are shepherds that cannot understand: they all look to their own way, every one for his gain, from his quarter. *Isaiah 56:11*

For I was envious at the foolish, when I saw the prosperity of the wicked. *Psalm 73:3*

So are the ways of every one that is greedy of gain; which taketh away the life of the owners thereof. *Proverbs 1:19*

He that is greedy of gain troubleth his own house; but he that hateth gifts shall live. *Proverbs 15:27*

Such ugly terminology is used in the Bible on the subject of greed. I believe it is because God unselfishly gives us grace, mercy and blessings regularly. He owns the whole world and allows us to share in His wealth. We should be grateful for the pieces of silver that we have. Most importantly, we must remember that He gave his only son to die in our place. Jesus' blood was the only currency that could "pay" our way into Heaven.

What do you have an insatiable need for?

_____

_____

_____

_____

_____

Did your childhood influence your need to want more and more?

_____

_____

_____

_____

What actions can you take to replace your desire to own possessions with a desire to surrender your will to God?

_____

_____

_____

_____

_____

Not that I speak in respect of want: for I have learned, in whatsoever state I am, therewith to be content. *Philippians 4:11*

+ Now, spend a few moments praying for freedom from your negative feeling.

Uncharitable

Selfish

Unable to show mercy

Unwilling to share

It may be true that you spent years waking up early and staying up late. Or, you may have been born with a head start. Someone in the generations before rose early and toiled into the evening.

But the question is this: Who really paid the price for you to enjoy your life? The answer is: Jesus. He died upon the cross for your sin and my sin.

First of all, you cannot keep it all. The government will get some of it. You cannot will 100% of it to your children and you can't take it with you.

For we brought nothing into this world, and it is certain we can carry nothing out *1 Timothy 6:7*

Secondly, when we refuse to help others, we fail to give God glory.

And the King shall answer and say unto them, Verily I say unto you, Inasmuch as ye have done it unto one of the least of these my brethren, ye have done it unto me. *Matthew 25:40*

Then shall he answer them, saying, Verily I say unto you, Inasmuch as ye did it not to one of the least of these, ye did it not to me. *Matthew 25:45*

Woe unto you, scribes and Pharisees, hypocrites! for ye devour widows' houses, and for a pretence make long prayer: therefore ye shall receive the greater damnation. *Matthew 23:14*

Read 1 Timothy, chapters five and six about responsibilities of men and the church. The state of the world shows that we are off track.

MEDITATION

In the scripture from the Gospel of Matthew listed above, Jesus was angry with the Pharisees (church goers) who took advantage of people. Why was it such an abomination?

_____

_____

_____

_____

_____

How can you become more charitable?

_____

_____

_____

_____

_____

_____

How is helping others, honoring God?

_____

_____

_____

_____

MEMORY VERSE

For the love of money is the root of all evil: which while some coveted after, they have erred from the faith, and pierced themselves through with many sorrows. *1 Timothy 6:10*

+ Now, spend a few moments praying for freedom from your negative feeling.

Trapped

Enslaved

Unable to be free

We are free. That is just the plain truth. We are not prisoners of our circumstance. Although we may be in a holding pattern, God is in charge of our flight.

Talk with him about the delay. Be still and know that He is God and He is in complete control. He may be waiting on your conversation. He may be waiting on your growth. He may be waiting on another person to become ready. Whatever it is, He is working on your behalf.

In the meantime, remain confident that you are NOT trapped!

And ye shall know the truth, and the truth shall make you free.
John 8:32

If the Son therefore shall make you free, ye shall be free indeed.
John 8:36

Being justified freely by his grace through the redemption that is in Christ Jesus: ***Romans 3:24***

Now we have received, not the spirit of the world, but the spirit which is of God; that we might know the things that are freely given to us of God. ***1 Corinthians 2:12***

What has made you feel trapped?

_____

_____

_____

_____

_____

If you love the Lord and are striving to be a Christ-centered person, you need to remember that God is always working on your behalf and waiting for an appointed time to deliver you. With that in mind, what do you believe He is doing, right now?

_____

_____

_____

_____

_____

One of the blessings from God each day is His love. His love is beautiful but it is also powerful. When you reveal to God an open channel in which he can operate, you will not feel trapped. What can you do whenever you feel trapped to bring His presence into your room, into your mind and into your heart?

_____

_____

_____

_____

_____

Stand fast therefore in the liberty wherewith Christ hath made us free, and be not entangled again with the yoke of bondage. *Galatians 5:1*

+ Now, spend a few moments praying for freedom from your negative feeling.

The Fruit of the Spirit

I am the vine, ye are the branches: He that abideth in me, and I in him, the same bringeth forth much fruit: for without me ye can do nothing. *John 15:5*

We are to represent Christ. He is the vine and our character should be the representative fruit of the loving wonderful vine that is JESUS!

But the fruit of the Spirit is love, joy, peace, longsuffering (patience), gentleness, goodness, faith, Meekness (humility), temperance (self-control)...If we live in the Spirit, let us also walk in the Spirit. *Galatians 5:22-23, 25*

The Christian lifestyle requires the ability to differentiate. We must accept that there are two realms that exist – the spiritual realm and the natural realm. We must be able to take steps by faith and not by what we see before us. We must wait for the manifestation. Romans 4:17 tells us that God can call those things that have not happened as though they are already presently existing. With the Lord, we are strong enough to fight.

Use this devotion to wage war on your thoughts. Our thoughts can weaken us, cripple us, and lock us in an invisible prison. Free yourself. Pray earnestly. Fight valiantly. Love God boldly. Live blessed. -VH

Made in the USA
Columbia, SC
07 November 2017